STADT Wien
BEKANNT

STADT Wien BEKANNT

Useless Facts
Vienna

Holzbaum

Stadtbekannt Medien GmbH Useless Facts Vienna www.stadtbekannt.at
1. Edition 2014 ISBN 978-3-902980-10-6
Photos Stadtbekannt Medien GmbH (unless otherwise indicated)
Photographers Calina Fontanesi and Marlene Mautner
Translator Domenik Pockberger
Print Theiss, St. Stefan in Lavanttal

TABLE OF CONTENTS

PREFACE

„Wien, Wien, nur du allein..." (Only You, Vienna), goes a popular Viennese song about this charming city by the Danube River. Its moving history, its vibrant culture, the legendary Viennese snide humor – Vienna is more than a city, Vienna is a way of life.

STADTBEKANNT has become completely immersed in this way of life and Vienna's unique atmosphere, and we wanted to share our joy with others. When coming up with ideas on how to present this beautiful city, how to capture its genuine spirit to give you a sense of what Vienna is about, we had a revelation.

To appreciate how "leiwand" (great) Vienna really is and always has been, one has to indulge in the irrelevant facts, the useless information. The soul of Vienna consists of those seemingly marginal notes, those amusing anecdotes, bizarre characters, traditional customs and oddities, which are nowhere to be found in today's history books and travels guides.

This book is a collection of all the useless facts, all those Vienna-curious, Vienna-connoisseurs, and Vienna-philes don't necessarily need to know, but probably want to know.

We hope you enjoy this declaration of love to this wonderful city.

HISTORICAL NONSENSE

Vienna is a city full of moving history and anecdotes. Why the State Opera House is sinking, how city hall tricked a church, and why the Vienna Supper is superior to the Last Supper, is answered in this chapter.

St. Francis of Assisi Church on Mexico Square

MEXICO SQUARE

The square's name commemorates the fact that Mexico was the only country that opposed Austria's annexation to the Third Reich in the League of Nations in 1938.

KÄRNTNER STREET

Kärntner Street, which was first documented as "Strata Carinthianorum" in 1257, was originally planned as a highway in the Middle Ages. It ran

KÄRNTNER STREET
With around 125,000 people, Kärntner Street is the second most frequented shopping street after the Graben.

from the city center to the city walls and along its extensions, Triester Street and Venediger Street, all the way through the State of Carinthia to Trieste and Venice respectively.

NEGERDÖRFL (NEGRO VILLAGE)

I'M A NEGERANT, MISS! The adjective "neger" (span. negro, french. nègre from lat. niger) means being broke, bankrupt, insolvent. Black stands for bad luck, poverty, darkness, death, malice, danger, power. For obvious reasons, this expression is not used anymore.

The "Negerdörfl", a settlement built in 1911 between Kopp Street and Gablenz Street, quickly became the epitome of misery, immorality and crime.

THE TOWN OF LIESING

Liesing obtained city rights at the beginning of the 20th century. It is the only town within Vienna's city limits.

SCHLESINGER SQUARE

Anti-fascism made easy: In 2006, Schlesinger Square was renamed Schlesinger Square. It was originally named after Reichstag deputy Josef Schlesinger. Now, it commemorates social-democrat Therese Schlesinger.

NIBELUNGEN QUARTER

Some streets in the Nibelungen Quarter in the 15th district are named after creatures from the Song of the Nibelungs: Alberich Street, Brunhilden Street, Dankwart Street, Gernot Street, Giselher Street, Gunther Street, Hagen

Mariahilfer Street

Street, Kriemhild Square, Volker Street ...

MARIAHILFER STREET

Mariahilfer Street has had quite a lot of names throughout history: Kremser Street, Bavarian Street, Laimgrubner Main Street, Schönbrunn Lane, Mariahilfer Ground Street, Mariahilfer Main Street, Fünfhauser Main Street, Penzinger Postal Street, Schönbrunner Street, Penzinger Street.

SHOPPING STREET
The shops of the inner Mariahilfer Street have a total selling space of about 1,940,000 square feet (180,000 m^2). That roughly corresponds to the retail selling space of the entire inner city.

MAGDALENEN GROUNDS

The Magdalenen Grounds in the 6th district used to be called "The pigsty by the Wien river" and later "The rat-pit"

THE BRUNNEN MARKET

THE BRUNNEN MARKET is the longest year-round market in Europe and is also known as "Orient around the corner".

The Brunnen Market owes its name to a well (Brunnen) originally located there. The well eventually had to yield to technology and was

The Reichsbridge

torn down during the installation of the Horse Tramway.

THE REICHSBRIDGE

The Reichsbridge collapsed on August 1st 1976, the same day Niki Lauda crashed his Formula 1 car at the Nurembergring.

THE REICHSBRIDGE
Today's Reichsbridge is already the third bridge with the same name crossing the Danube. The first Reichsbridge was in use from 1876 to 1937, the second Reichsbridge from 1937 to 1976. The third Reichsbridge opened in 1980.

DER RATHAUSMANN (THE MAN OF CITY HALL)

CITY HALL TOWER
The "Rathausmann" (plus flag) is around 18 feet tall and weighs almost 4,000 pounds.

The main tower of city hall was not supposed to reach higher than the two towers of the Votiv Church. To surpass them anyway, the "Rathausmann" was placed on top of the tower.

THE GATE OF THE PREGNANT

ALSER CHURCH
Thanks to the orphanage, Alser Church is Europe's largest matrimonial archive. (Register of Baptisms, Nuptials and Deaths)

The gate of the "secretly pregnant" led to the delivery ward of the General Hospital (AKH), where single women could conceive children out of wedlock, and hand them over to the orphanage next door. Between 1784 and 1910, around 700,000 women have used these facilities.

MYSTERIOUS INSCRIPTION

GREEK QUARTER
In the heart of the Greek Quarter, on Greek Street 4, lies the so-called Styria Yard, which is, next to the Heumühle in Wieden, one of the oldest secular buildings in the city.

If you follow the Hafnersteig from Sweden Square to Greek Street and turn into the first house on the left, you will see two dark wooden boards. The Arabic letters inscribed here have long been a mystery and could not be translated. In 2007, the Orientalist Arne A. Ambros shed light on the subject. The inscription reads, "Arrange for a comfortable life and enjoy the pleasures that last".

Fool's Tower

PRICEY KIDNAPPING

While in 1971, 250,000 ATS was paid ransom for kidnapping victim Hans Bensdorf, the Schöps-kidnapping in 1976 cost 27,000,000 ATS. The Palmers-kidnapping, in 1977, tops the list with 31,000,000 ATS.

ATS
The international abbreviation for the Austrian Schilling, which was the national currency in Austria before the Euro, was "ATS". The exchange rate for 1 Euro was 13.7603 ATS.

FOOL'S TOWER

GUGLHUPF (Bundt cake)
Due to its shape, the Fool's Tower is also called "Guglhupf".

The Fool's Tower, built in 1784 on the grounds of the old General Hospital in the 9th district, was the first "madhouse" in the world.

SO MANY DEVILS

In 1583, sixteen-year old Anna Schluttenbauer was subjected to a public exorcism. Her ordeal was not in vain – as the legend goes, no less than 12,562 devils appeared.

WITCH TRIAL

WITCH TRIAL
The Elsa-Plainacher Street in Donaustadt remembers the victim of the witch hunt.

The only witch trial to ever take place in Vienna was the Elisabeth Plainacher case in 1583.

VIENNA CRIME GANGS

In the summer of 1905 , the newspaper "Das Illustrierte Wiener Extrablatt" reported on crime gangs in Vienna. It compared the "Beer Gang", the "G'stutzte Mirzl Gang", and the "Fetzer Gang" with the "Apaches" in Paris, the "Hooligans" in London and the "Mularias" from Trieste. The article concluded that all three cities suffered less crime in two months, than Vienna endured within the course of two days.

PUBLIC EXECUTIONS IN VIENNA

Am Tabor – Drownings
Weißgerberlände – Burned at the stake
Hoher Markt – Dismemberment and Decapitation
Spinnerin am Kreuz – Hangings and the Breaking Wheel
Rossau – Hangings and the Breaking Wheel

CEMETERY EXPRESS

To fast-track the transportation of corpses, the city once planned a cemetery express.

VIENNA CENTRAL CEMETERY
The "population" of this cemetery is around 3 million, which is about half the number of Vienna natives that have ever lived in Vienna.

THE GRAVEDIGGERS OF THE SCHWECHAT BREWERY

Until the beginning of the 20th century, almost 600 corpses were pulled out of the water in Kaiserebersdorf. For some reason, the workers at the beer plant in Schwechat were responsible for their burials.

JOSEF LANG

Josef Lang was the last executioner of the monarchy. After the suspension of the death penalty, he worked as a janitor on Gottschalk Street 1 in Simmering.

DEATH BY HANGING
As executioner of Vienna, Josef Lang hanged 39 people from 1900 to 1918 .

Parliament

RUMBLE IN THE PARLIAMENT

MARK TWAIN
Mark Twain lived somewhere in Vienna from September 28, 1897, to May 27, 1899.

The Imperial Assembly was the scene of regular fist fights. The wildest one happened on November 26, 1897. The reason was a decree, which required Austrian state workers in the Czech Republic to learn Czech. Despite police intervention, a massive brawl erupted. A famous

© Wiener Linien 01.04.1913

witness was watching from the stands. It was Mark Twain.

SEDAN

In 1780, the Fiaker (horse carriages) were competing for customers with around 100 public sedans (carrying chairs).

LEFT-HANDED TRAFFIC

Vienna carried left-handed traffic until 1938.

LEFT-HANDED TRAFFIC is carried in 59 countries with a combined 2.5 billion people.

© Wiener Linien 10.03.1963

CONDUCTOR-LESS

CONDUCTOR-LESS
WOLFANG AMBROS
nce, conductors used to impress,
Those days are over,
today we ride conductor-less."

The transition to trams without ticket collectors / conductors took over 32 years. On December 1, 1964, the first conductor-less tram (Line 43) started operating. The last tram with a conductor on board ran on December 20, 1996. The reason for this transition wasn't budget cuts, it was lack of human resources.

DOUBLE-DECKER BUS

From 1960 to 1991, the "Wiener Linien" (Vienna Lines) operated double-decker buses.

OMNIBUS DRIVERS

Originally, Vienna omnibus drivers were driving without a roof above their heads. This "custom" was adopted from the omnibuses' predecessors – the Viennese horse-carriages.

FIRST ROUNDABOUT

The first roundabout in Vienna was built around Michaeler Square in 1927.

ROUNDABOUTS
The Praterstern is the largest roundabout in Vienna. The Verteilerkreis Favoriten comes in second.

STREETLIGHTS

On November 27, 1962, at 4pm, Vienna's last gas lantern was extinguished on Saurau Street in Hietzing.

VIENNA STATE OPERA

Viennese people love nicknames: As "sunken jalopy" they once lovingly described their opera house – not without reason. During construction, Ring Street was raised about 3 feet, which made it look as if this magnificent building was swallowed by the earth. By the

BEEHIVE
Since 2010, there is a beehive with a population of around 60,000 bees on the roof of the Vienna State Opera.

Vienna State Opera
Architects August Sicard von Sicardsburg and Eduard van der Nüll

way, both architects died before its completion. Eduard van der Null couldn't handle the criticism and committed suicide. Two months later, August Sicard von Sicardsburg died of a heart attack.

VIENNA BOYS' CHOIR

CONCERTS
Each year, the Vienna Boys' choir performs around 300 concerts around the world.

The Vienna boys' Choir wears the coat of arms of Austria on their seamen outfits. The idea came from no other than Walt Disney.

Minoriten Church

THE VIENNA SUPPER

There is a perfect replica of the "Last Super" at Minoriten Church in Vienna. Not only is the mosaic, measuring 29 x 13 feet, in much better condition, it is also far more colorful than the one in Milan by Leonardo Da Vinci. The Viennese version has another significant advantage over the original: You can see Jesus' feet.

MINORITEN CHURCH
Originally, the painting was supposed to be exhibited at Belvedere Palace. It turned out to be too large and ended up at Minoriten Church.

MARCUS AURELIUS

Marcus Aurelius died on March 17, 180, in Vindobona (Vienna).

VIENNA SEWER SYSTEM

SEWERAGE
Up to 15 tons of sediment are removed from the sewers each day to keep the system running.

In 1739, Vienna was the first city in Europe to have comprehensive sewerage.

Elisabeth Bathory

ELISABETH BATHORY

Hungarian countess Elisabeth Bathory killed around 650 young girls to bathe in their blood. She believed that the blood of young girls would cure aging and took regular blood showers in her palace on Augustiner Street. Rumor has it that her story was the inspiration for Bram Stoker's Dracula.

INSPIRATION
The blood countess inspired the work of numerous Black metal bands. British band Venom dedicated the song "Countess Bathory" to her, Swedish band "Bathory" named itself after the countess, the band "Die Untoten" released the album "The Blood Countess" in 2006, and German dark metal band "Nachtblut" wrote a song, also titled "The Blood Countess".

HEDY LAMARR

HEAVEN
After Hedy Lamarr's death, one half of her ashes was spread at a place called "Am Himmel" (In Heaven) in the Vienna Woods.

Viennese actor Hedy Lamarr and composer George Antheil invented the spread spectrum technique. The technique is still used today in telecommunication for blue-tooth and GSM. On November 9, Inventor's Day is celebrated in the honor of Hedy Lamarr.

THE BEAUTIFUL LISL GOLDARBEITER

To this day, Lisl Goldarbeiter remains Austria's only Miss Universe. In 1929, she was voted Miss Austria in Vienna. That same year, she was crowned Miss Universe in Texas.

RHEE FRANCESCA

NAME
Despite being named Franziska at birth, she later changed the spelling of her name to both, Franzeska or Francesca.

Rhee Francesca, wife of president Rhee-Syngman and the very first First Lady of South Korea from 1948 to 1961, was born as Franziska Donner, daughter of sparkling-water factory owner Josef Donner from Inzersdorf. The people of Korea nick-named Lady Francesca "Hojudaek" - "The woman from Australia"

Chairs in the park

CHAIR-LADIES

Sitting down wasn't always free. Until the 1950's, so-called "Chair-ladies" rented out chairs in parks across Vienna.

THE WHITE WOMAN

The white woman, legendary ghost of the Vienna Hofburg Palace, was last sighted in 1898. It was never established, if she wore white or black gloves with her white dress.

GLOVES
White gloves stand for joyous events, black gloves symbolize calamities.

COPA CAGRANA AND THE FRANZ-JOSEFS-LAND

Name-giving Vienna Style: Before the Copa Cagrana existed, there was the near by "Franz-Josef's-Land" - a gastronomical area, named after the polar islands with restaurants like "Zum Nordpol" (Northpole)

WATER-PROOF MASCARA

FORMULA
It took Winterstein-Kambersky over 2,000 trials to find the right formula for her invention.

Viennese singer Helene Winterstein-Kambersky invented the first water-proof mascara in 1920.

Scycraper Herren Street

VIENNA'S OLDEST SKYSCRAPER

In 1931/32, Vienna's first skyscraper was built on Herren Street. With the rise of surrounding structures, it is barely noticed today. Back then, resident protests limited the building's height to 164 feet spanning over 16 floors.

SCYSCRAPER HERREN STREET
Herren Street 6-8
Fahnen Street 2
Wallner Street 5-7
1010 Vienna

TOOTHPASTE FROM LIESING

Toothpaste in the tube was invented in Liesing.

In 1887, Liesing based company F.A. Sarg's Sohn & Co. manufactured the first toothpaste in the tube called "Kalodont".

VIENNA CITY WALL

In 1858, the slighting of Vienna's city wall began. Its entire destruction took 15 years. Close to 1,000 homes were built almost simultaneously in its place.

CITY GATES
Before the city wall was removed, the following city gates existed: Rotenturmgate, Fischergate, Neugate, Schottengate, Franzensgate, Burggate, New Kärntner Gate, Kärntnergate, Old Kärntner Gate, Karolinengate, Stubengate, Franz-Josefs-Gate.

Otto Wagner Church

OTTO WAGNER CHURCH

It's not a coincidence that Otto Wagner Church is built on the grounds of the insane asylum "Steinhof". After numerous protests against the church's simplistic architecture, its construction was moved to the grounds of the asylum.

STEINHOF
Despite its actual name, Church of St. Leopold, the church at "Steinhof" is commonly known as Otto Wagner Church.

STOSS (PUSH)

In 1970, the average rent for a backroom, which hosted the card game "Stoß", was 2,000 ATS per hour. Rough estimates suggest a revenue of around 3 million ATS per night.

STOSS
The cardgame Stoß is also known under the names "Meine Tante" (My Aunt), "Deine Tante" (Your Aunt) or "Naschi Waschi". In the US it may be called "Stuss" or "Jewish Faro".

VENICE IN VIENNA

In 1895, "Venice in Vienna" opened at the Prater on today's Kaiserwiese. The replica of the city of Venice covered several thousand square feet and was one of the first theme parks in the world. Today, the street name Venediger Au is the only reminder of its former glory, the channels, the Palazzi, and the Gondolieri.

THEME PARKS
After only 5 years, the people of Vienna lost interest. In 1901, "Venice in Vienna" was replaced by "International city", then came "Flower city", followed by "Electric city" in 1903.

A·MARIA·THERESIA·E
PERFECIT·A

IMPERIAL SECRETS

No one embodies Austria‘s monarchy as much as Franz and Sisi, whose portrayal in the famous “Sissi” films was so unbelievably innocent and full of harmony. Why Kaiserin Sisi (Empress Elisabeth) would run into problems with today‘s drug laws, why Vienna‘s prostitutes had a beef with King Joseph II., and numerous fun facts about Schönbrunn Palace, Hofburg Palace and the House of Habsburg, you will find in this chapter.

© Schloß Schönbrunn
Kultur- und Betriebsges.m.b.H.

SISI'S TATTOO

On one of her many travels, Sisi – Empress Elisabeth – got a tattoo of an anchor on her shoulder.

SISI MUSEUM
Hofburg Palace
Michaeler Dome
1010 Vienna

COCAINE FOR THE EMPRESS

Empress Elizabeth's first-aid travel kit usually contained a "cocain syringe", as well as a "cocaine bottle". The syringe wasn't unusual for the times. Back then, cocaine was a popular medicine to cure ailments like sore throat. Cocaine candy, for example, was given to teething kids.

SISI LOVED VEILCHEN EIS (VIOLET ICE CREAM)

Sisi loved frozen food. Her beloved violet ice cream was an important part of her daily diet, which consisted mainly of meat broth. Every once in a while, the empress squeezed in a fruit day.

IMPERIAL FOLDING

THE SILVER COLLECTION
Hofburg Palace
Michaeler Dome
1010 Vienna

Imperial folding was only to be used at official dinners in the presence of the Emperor. It required for an Emperor Roll or a Pretzel stick to be placed in the vault of the napkin.

The folding technique remains a well kept secret to this day. Only 2 people know about it. It is still the highlight of every state dinner hosting crowned monarchs or presidents.

EMPRESS ELIZABETH'S MANE

Sisi, Empress of Austria and fashion icon, grew her hair so long, it reached all the way to the ground. It was combed for two hours each day. The Empress used these hair-sessions to learn foreign languages.

© Schloß Schönbrunn Kultur- und Betriebsges.m.b.H. Foto: Julius Silver

SCHÖNBRUNN YELLOW

SCHÖNBRUNN PALACE
www.schoenbrunn.at

After a string of color mishaps (at one point the color was rose), Schönbrunn Palace now shines in Schönbrunn yellow. However, the rich and earthy yellow is not the real Schönbrunn yellow. The recent renovation of the facade revealed, that the actual yellow is much brighter.
Since the monarchy spanned from Hungary to Moldava, state buildings, modeled after the ones in Vienna, were also painted yellow.

The Habsburg family's expansive marriage

politics exported the Schönbrunn yellow all the way to Brazil. After Archduchess Mary-Leopoldine of Habsburg, daughter of Emperor Franz I., was married to Prince Dom Pedro in December 1822, she was ex officio Empress of Brazil – which is why the Schönbrunn yellow can be found in the Brazilian national flag.

FAN LANGUAGE

During the Baroque and Rokoko period, hand-fans were used as a form of sign-language – to ask someone out for a date in the park, for example.

SCHÖNBRUNN PALACE

After the construction of the water basin and the fountains at the Imperial Gardens, it turned out that there wasn't enough water available. Twelve, already completed basins had to be covered up again.

SCHÖNBRUNN PALACE
www.schoenbrunn.at

SECRET CONFERENCES

Inside the circular Chinese Cabinet (there is an oval one as well), Maria Theresa held secret state conferences and discussions with Prime Minister Prince Kaunitz. Both cabinets were also used by the Empress to wallow in her passion for gambling.

MANDARINES, LEMONS AND ORANGES

The Austrian State Garden's collection of citrus fruits consists of 400 different plants. The valuable collection contains numerous historical plants, among them specimen up to 180 years old.

Part of the collection is open to the public during the summer months at the Crown Prince Garden at Schönbrunn Palace. Citrus fruits have been cultivated in the Imperial Gardens since 1647.

Berglroom © Schloß Schönbrunn Kultur- und Betriebsges.m.b.H., Photographer: Peter Olschinsky

JOHANN BAPTIST WENZEL BERGL

BERGLROOM
After its renovation, the impressive wall paintings in the Berglroom, inside the Crown Prince- and the Goess-apartments, are now open to the public (reservation required).

Johann Baptist Wenzel Bergl, one of Empress Maria-Theresa's favorite painters, created the wall paintings inside her private apartment at Schönbrunn Palace around 1770. He is responsible for the Berglrooms (known as the Gisela Apartments), the Goess- and the Crown Prince apartment.

© Schloß Schönbrunn Kultur- und Betriebsges.m.b.H.

GLORIETTE

The Gloriette, which is on the grounds of Schönbrunn Palace, offers a stunning view of the Palace itself and the city of Vienna.

GLORIETTE
The Gloriette, which is on the grounds of Schönbrunn Palace, offers a stunning view of the Palace itself and the city of Vienna.

VIENNESE ENDING

Emperor Joseph II. issued a decree, banning sad theater plays to avoid putting the Imperial crowd in a bad mood. A lot of plays had to be rewritten to provide them with a so-called

Viennese ending, which is basically a Happy Ending. Plays like “Romeo and Juliet” or “Hamlet”, for example, were given an alternative ending.

LABYRINTH

LABYRINTH
Schönbrunn Palace
www.schoenbrunn.at

Around 1720, a labyrinth was built at the Imperial Gardens. After re-opening in 1999, the labyrinth, which is modeled after the original, received two healing stones which were activated by Feng-Shui masters Jes and Julie Lim.

Hofburg

AUDIENCE

Emperor Franz-Joseph granted around 260,000 people an audience. He often welcomed more than 100 people a day in his audience chamber at Hofburg Palace.

IMPERIAL APARTMENTS
Hofburg Palace
Michaeler Dome
1010 Vienna
www.hofburg-wien.at

VIENNA HOFBURG PALACE

Hofburg Palace has 18 sections, 19 courtyards and around 2,600 rooms.

SISSI TRILOGY

SISSI IN THE MOVIES
An on-going exhibition shows the original set-designs from the Sissi films and reveals interesting information about actors and film locations.

Hofmobiliendepot
Andreasgasse 7
1070 Vienna
www.hofmobiliendepot.at

The Sissi film trilogy by Ernst Marischka was mostly filmed at Liechtenstein City Palace, using set-designs from the State's Personal Property Administration, as authentic locations either weren't available or restricted from filming.

HABSBURG GIBLETS

AUGUSTINER CHURCH
Augustiner Street 3
1010 Vienna

STEPHANSDOM
Stephan's Square 1
1010 Vienna

KAPUZINER CHURCH
Tegetthoff Street 2
1010 Vienna

An old Habsburg funeral procedure requires the heart and the intestines to be buried separate from the body. The heart was usually stored inside a silver container in the Heart tomb of Loreto Chapel at Augustiner Church. The intestines ended up in the Duke's tomb in the catacombs underneath St. Stephan's Cathedral. The corpse was laid to rest inside the Kapuziner tomb at Kapuziner Church.

THERE GOES THE EMPEROR ...

The restaurant "Witwe Bolte" on Gutenberg Street 13, around Spittelberg, has an inscription on the outside wall that reads,"Through this gate, the emperor came flying..." The story goes that Emperor Joseph II. was thrown out of a brothel there, because he was too stingy.

MOZART

MUSICAL NOTES

Michael Jackson wrote a song here, the Vienna Philharmonic is more than just an orchestra, and one famous composer had his brain picked even after his death. Vienna is the city of music. What you didn't know about Vienna's musical soul – and probably never wanted to know – we have gathered for you with plenty of rhythm.

Johann Strauss Jr.

JOHANN STRAUSS JR.

The waltz "Faschings-Lieder" (Carneval songs) by Johann Strauss Jr. had its successful premiere at the Casino Dommayer in Hietzing, the same place he made his debut on October 15, 1844.

NICKNAME
Friends and family called Johann Strauss "Schani".

FRANZ SCHUBERT

Franz Schubert allegedly never took off his glasses, not even at night time.

ARNOLD SCHÖNBERG

WATSCHENKONZERT (SLAP-IN-THE-FACE CONCERT)
In 1913, a fight broke out at the Vienna Musikverein between followers of Schönberg and his opponents. The scandal became known as the "Watschenkonzert".

The composer from Vienna suffered from Triskaidekaphobie, the fear of the number 13. He was born on a 13th and actually died on a Friday the 13th.

JOSEF HAYDN'S STOLEN HEAD

PASSIONATE FISHERMAN
Joseph Haydn loved to fish.

At the time of Josef Haydn's death, Napoleons troops were occupying the city, which is why this musical genius couldn't be buried properly. When his tomb was exhumed 15 years later to move him to a different tomb, his head was missing. Craniology supporters had stolen it and after a few detours, it ended up in the hands of the "Gesellschaft der Musikfreunde in Wien" (Society of Friends of the Music in Vienna). It wasn't until 1954, for the head to return to its rightful owner.

MUSICAL BANK ROBBERY

ALLGEMEINE VERUNSICHERUNG
Only one member, Thomas Spitzer, remains of the original band.

On February 27, 2007, hostages were taken during a bank robbery. To alert authorities, a neighbor living across the street, blasted the hit-song "Banküberfall" (Bankrobbery).

Street sign Falcostiege

FALCO

Falco named himself after the ski-jumper Falko Weißpflog.

HANS HÖLZEL

By receiving the City of Vienna's badge of merit in 1986, Hans Hölzel (also known as Falco) became the youngest recipient at the age of 29.

FALCO IMITATOR
Michael Patrik Simoner is the only Falco imitator officially recognized by the Falco foundation.

DER KOMMISSAR (THE INSPECTOR)

KOTTAN INVESTIGATES
In episode 11 of the popular crime series "Kottan investigates", Falco played a stand-in pianist in inspector Kottan's police band.

After the release of the single "Der Kommisar" by the first, white rapper Falco, three bars in Los Angeles were renamed "Der Kommissar".

MICHAEL JACKSON

Michael Jackson wrote his song "Earth Song" at the Imperial Hotel in Vienna.

Art History Museum, Architect Gottfried Semper

LOOS BAR

The manager of Guns'N'Roses wanted to reserve seats for the band, crew and roadies (around 60 people) at this legendary bar, but was quickly turned down by barman Roberto. The reason: The bar is only about 290 square feet small.

KILL BILL 2
Quentin Tarantino fell in love with a woman he met at Loos Bar, and named a character after her in the movie Kill Bill 2.

SEMPER DEPOT

GOTTFRIED SEMPER
Architects Gottfried Semper and Carl Freiherr von Hasenauer built the Semper Depot, the New Hofburg Palace, the Natural History Museum, the Art History Museum and the Vienna State Theater.

Robbie Williams' video for his song "Lovelight" was filmed at the Semper Depot in Mariahilf.

THE VIENNESE YODEL

The Viennese yodel is, contrary to traditional yodeling, performed inside. In 2010, the Viennese yodel was added to the List of Intangible Cultural Heritage by the UNESCO.

GOOD EVENING, MR. WALDHEIM

US-singer Lou Reed wrote a song called "Good evening, Mr. Waldheim" (a former president of Austria). The song is an ironic take on political relations and their prominent figures.

BIG PHIL

VIENNA PHILHARMONIC
For the presentation of the coin on Riesenrad Square at the Wiener Prater, the Giant Ferris Wheel was turned into a huge Philharmonic coin.

The Big Phil, an anniversary edition of the Vienna Philharmonic coin, is valued at 100,000 Euro and considered legal tender. If you are thinking of a shopping spree, think again. The coin weighs 60 pounds and its value of raw materials is around 1,300,000.00 Euro.

OLIVER OTTITSCH
GAY NAZI DOLPHINS AT A GANG BANG
CARTOONS
Holzbaum

CULINARY BITES

Vienna is a town of culinary indulgence. There is never a bad time to eat a Schnitzel, sip on a Kapuziner or nourish those love handles with a Sacher-Torte. The following chapter provides all the useless information necessary about Viennese delicacies, culinary delights and Pub-culture.

Cappuccino

FROM KAPUZINER TO CAPPUCCINO

The Viennese coffee drink "Kapuziner", named after the hood (Kapuze) of the Kapuziner order, was the blueprint for the Cappuccino, which was invented in Italy as an improvement to the Kapuziner.

COFFEE
In the Viennese coffeehouse tradition there are about 50 different ways to make coffee, depending on the size and shape of the cup or glass, as well as the use of condiments (cream, whipped cream, milk, milk foam, sugar or alcohol).

THE FIRST ESPRESSO MACHINE

Austria's first Espresso machine operated in a Vienna coffeehouse on Wollzeile. A branch of the pastry chain Aida delighted Vienna coffee lovers with this novelty.

Cafe Griensteidl, Photographer: Carl von Zamboni

CAFE GRIENSTEIDL

VIENNA COFFEE HOUSE TRADITION
In 2011, the Viennese coffeehouse tradition was added to UNESCO's List of Intangible Cultural Heritage.

In the 19th century, Cafe Griensteidl, in the first district, was also known as "Cafe Größenwahn" (Cafe Megalomania), because of its clientele.

TURKISH BAGEL

The shape of a bagel looks a bit like a stirrup. Rumor has it, that this biscuit pays homage to the Polish King Jan Sobieski, who sent horsemen to help fight the Turkish army during the second siege of Vienna.

Swedish Bombs

SWEDISH BOMBS

Walter Niemetz, a pastry manufacturer in Vienna, had a friend from Sweden. To remember his friend, he created a pastry called "The Swedish Bomb".

600 Swedish Bombs are manufactured every minute. One half of the chocolate coated bombs gets coconut flakes sprinkled on top.

SACHER-TORTE (SACHER CAKE)

The largest "Original Sacher-Torte" ever baked

was 6,5 feet in diameter.

INVENTION OF THE SACHER-TORTE

In 1832, Prince Metternich ordered his chefs to create an exceptional dessert. Since the master chef was sick that day, his apprentice Franz Sacher completed the task and invented the Sacher-Torte.

KRAPFEN (FILLED DONUTS)

In the 19th century, it was Viennese custom to ask someone out for a "Krapfen". The girl broke the "Krapfen" in half and shared it with the boy. This was a sign of engagement.

APRICOT JAM
In Vienna, all "Krapfen" have to be filled with apricot jam. Any other filling has to be labeled as such.

OWANES ASTOUATZATUR

In 1685, Owanes Astouatzatur, also known as Diodato, opened the first Viennese coffeehouse at the Haar Market, today's Rotenturm Street 14.

ICE CREAM

In 1865, the first ice cream manufacturer arrived in Vienna from Cadore. He sold ice cream at the Vienna Prater. From here, ice cream manufacturers from the north of Italy eventually conquered all of central Europe.

TICHY

In 1967, Kurt Tichy invented the frozen apricot dumpling.

EDEN BAR

In 2004, the legendary Eden Bar celebrated its 100th birthday. This seems strange, considering the building on Lilien Street by architect Rudolf Erdös was only built in 1911.

Wiener Schnitzel

RESTAURANT CHAIN “WIENERWALD”

SCHNITZ'L LAND
Today, there are five Wienerwald branches in Vienna. Since 2010, the company is run by the Schnitz'l Land company.

In 1978, this restaurant chain had 1,600 branches with over 30,000 employees all over the world.

THE WIENER SCHNITZEL

Just so you know, a Wiener Schnitzel has 518 Calories. It takes about 8 hours of sleep to burn this amount of calories.

Wertheim Palace on Schwarzenberg Square

THE FIRST MCDONALD'S IN VIENNA

The first McDonald's opened on July 27, 1977, at Wertheim Palace on Schwarzenberg Square.

VIENNA SAUSAGES

Original Vienna sausages are called "Frankfurter" in Vienna, as they originated in Frankfurt, Germany. The Wiener Schnitzel is called "Cololetta Milanese" in Milan, Italy, where the meat-dish has its roots. The Linzer cake is named after Viennese pastry chef Linzer.

NEULERCHENFELD – THE LARGEST TAVERN

WINE BAR "SITTL"
The wine bar "Sittl's" actual name is "The Golden Pelican tavern".

At the beginning of the 19th century, Neulerchenfeld was known as the largest tavern of the Holy Roman Empire. Back then, there was a tavern in 103 out of the 150 buildings. The wine bar "Sittl" is a reminder of those days.

STRANDBAR HERRMANN (HERRMANN'S BEACH BAR)

Strandbar Herrmann owes its name to professor Emanuel Herrmann, who invented the postcard.

VIENNESE CUISINE

The Viennese cuisine is the only cuisine named after a city.

Nussdorf, Vineyard

VITICULTURE

Around 585 hectare of land are dedicated to wine-growing in Vienna, making it the city with the largest urban vineyard acreage in the world.

VIENNESE WINE
Around 640 wine-growers produce more than half a million gallons of wine each year.

SCHANIGARTEN (SIDEWALK SEATING)

Johann "Gianni" Taroni was the first to obtain permission to put tables and chairs in front of his coffee shop on the Graben. Over time, the expression "Gianni's Garten" turned into "Schanigarten".

SCHANIGARTEN vs. GASTGARTEN (Sidewalk seating vs. Outdoor seating)
A Schanigarten is set up on public property, while a Gastgarten occupies private property. Today, there are over 1.800 Schanigärten and over 600 Gastgärten in Vienna.

VIENNESE WINE

VINEYARDS
Nussdorf, Heiligenstadt, Grinzing, Sievering, Salmannsdorf, Neustift am Walde, Mauer, Oberlaa, Stammersdorf, Strebersdorf, Jedlersdorf

The vintage of 1456 is said to have been so sour, the people of Vienna poured the wine into the streets. To avoid further spillage, Emperor Friedrich III. ordered the wine to be puddled with the mortar used to build the North Tower of St. Stephan's Cathedral.

VIENNA'S SMALLEST VINEYARD

Vienna's smallest vineyard is located on Schwarzenberg Square.

Water

WIENER BLUT (VIENNESE BLOOD)

This Viennese liqueur will give you hot flashes: red, hot chilli peppers give the "Wiener Blut" its luminous, red color, its strong bouquet, and intense, spicy flavor. Even more intimidating: 56% alcohol.

"Wiener Blut" is the title of a musical comedy (operetta) by Johann Strauß, a film by Willi Forst, an album and song by Falco, a book about Vienna's underworld by Robert Geher, a song by Rammstein, ...

WIENER AUSTERN (VIENNA OYSTERS)

"Wiener Austern" were sold by the "snail ladies" at the snail market. Until the beginning of the 20th century, Vienna was the Mecca of snail-lovers.

THE BURGUNDY SNAIL
The Burgundy snail was popular during Lenten season and because of its aphrodisiac effects.

SCHÖNBRUNN PALACE WATER

"Schönbrunn Palace water" is available at the store. However, it's from Styria, not from Schönbrunn Palace.

BAUCHERL (BELLY)

In Vienna, Coke with Brandy is called a "Baucherl" - because of the belly-shaped Brandy glass.

HESPERIDES' VINEGAR

In 1927, the company Mautner Markhof invented the Hesperides' vinegar, which is a mixture of distilled vinegar, wine vinegar and apple juice.

Useless Facts Vienna

www.facebook.com/uselessfactsvienna

ANIMAL DIRT

Vienna is not necessarily the lung of Austria, but the variety of the city‘s urban species is still quite impressive. How special the bond between pets and their owners, and the things they leave behind, can be, why shooting ducks year-round is prohibited, even though hunting is legal, and how to have a bit of “elephant luck”, you will learn in this chapter.

Elephants

ELEPHANT LITTER

The elephants at the Schönbrunn Zoo produce 30 buckets of litter every day. It is sold as fertilizer under the name "elephant luck". One bucket costs around 3.50 Euros.

ELEPHANT LUCK
The elephants at Vienna Zoo are named Drumbo, Kibo, Mongu, Numbi and Tonga.

HUNTING IN VIENNA

The state of Vienna is divided into 5 hunting districts. Around 1,500 members of the State's hunting association are licensed to hunt. According to the municipal department, 374 deer and 246 hares were shot in 2012.

VIENNESE DOGS RULE

COMPULSORY REGISTRATION
There are 57,000 dogs registered in Vienna.

There are 160 dog-zones available for the 57,000 dogs living in Vienna. 70 of those are equipped with a drinking trough. In Berlin, only 30, sometimes fee-based, dog-zones cater to over 100,000 dogs.

WORM DOCTOR

MUSEUM OF NATURAL HISTORY VIENNA
Burgring 7, 1010 Vienna
www.nhm-wien.ac.at

General practitioner Johann Gottfried Bremser dissected roughly 60,000 worms at the beginning of the 19th century. Because of his passion, Vienna's Museum of Natural History now boasts one of the oldest and largest collections of parasitical worms in the world.

VIENNA ANIMAL CEMETERY

The first animal cemetery in Vienna opened only a few years back, in November 2011.

WINKER FROGS (WAVING FROGS)

Schönbrunn Sensation! The Zoo Vienna was the first in the world to successfully breed Winker frogs. These frogs communicate, as their name suggests, by waving to one another.

Pigeons

PIGEONS IN VIENNA

A decree by the municipal administration of Vienna prohibits the shooting of pigeons within urban areas.

VIENNA PIGEONS

Vienna Shorty, Viennese Whiteshield, Vienna peewit, Vienna Röserlscheck, Vienna tumbler, Vienna highflyer and Old-Vienna highflyer are Vienna's domestic pigeons. The domestic pigeon is the domesticated version of the rock pigeon, which is part of the Columba species.

TURTLE DOVE
Closed season for Turtle doves is between April 11 and August 31.

The feral domesticated pigeon is called the street pigeon. With a population of roughly 150,000 street pigeons, Vienna ranks among the highest in Europe. Since not everyone seems to appreciate this achievement, the city has been quite creative to try and reduce the number of street pigeons – Contraceptive pills, falcons, pigeon hotels at the outskirts of Vienna, strategic deployment of pigeon egg dummies.

BATS

THE REVENGE OF THE BAT
The bat aka Dr. Falke is a character in the famous operetta "Die Rache der Fledermaus" (The Bat).

There are 20 types of bats in Vienna: the lesser horseshoe bat, the Daubenton's bat, the whiskered bat, the Nymph's bat, the Natterer's bat, the Geoffroy's bat, the Bechstein's bat, the Greater Mouse-eared bat, the common noctule bat, the Leisler bat, the common pipistrelle bat, the soprano pipistrelle bat, the Nathusius pipistrelle bat, the Kuhl's pipistrelle bat, the Savi's pipistrelle bat, the leather-winged bat, the serotine bat, the barbastelle bat, the common long-eared bat, the grey long-eared bat.

WILDLIFE CONQUERS THE CITY

VIENNESE FOXES
For years now, Vienna is the city with the highest quality of living – that includes wildlife: An estimated 4,000 foxes live within Vienna's city limits.

Somewhere between high-rises and highways, wild boars, foxes, and birds of prey roam the streets of Vienna. Back when humans were still a part of the food chain, they knew exactly which animals they couldn't escape from.

Bee

Here's a quick reminder: Rat 6.2 mph, Bear 31 mph, Fox 31 mph, Boar 34 mph, Wolf 40 mph.

BEETOWN VIENNA

Each year, around 200 million bees spend their summer in Vienna.

URBAN BEE-KEEPER
Around 600 beekeepers take care of the 5,300 permanent bee-colonies in Vienna.

VIENNESE EMPEROR

The Viennese Emperor is the largest European moth with around 6.6 inches. It does not eat. Its sole purpose is to reproduce.

WIENER (VIENNESE)

KEEPING PETS
Not just rabbits count as pets. Camels and water buffaloes are among the types of pets allowed in Vienna.

The White Wiener, the Blue Wiener, the Grey Wiener, the Grey-blue Wiener and the Black Wiener are all part of the Wiener species, which is its own, independent rabbit species.

SOLIMAN

On March 6, 1552, Soliman arrived in Vienna. He was a gift of Johanna, daughter of Emperor Karl V. and Isabella of Portugal, to Emperor Maximilian II. The 6th of March would go down in history, as Soliman was the first elephant to set foot in Vienna. After his death, his bones were crafted into a chair, which is still in the hands of the Diocese Kremsmünster, as well as smaller furniture like cane- or umbrella stands. Soliman was preserved and ended up in the Bavarian National Museum (where it rotted inside a damp basement).

CAT LITTER

30,000 tons of cat litter ends up in Vienna's garbage each year.

VIENNESE DOGS

Dog-haters and dog-lovers beware: Donaustadt has the most dogs with a number of 7,012. Josefstadt has the fewest dogs with only 463.

RUN-FREE ZONE
With just over 10 square feet, the 7th district has the smallest allotment for dogs to run free. The second district offers the largest allotment with almost 1,400 square feet.

VIENNA'S DOG DIRT

Around 50,000 dog dirt bags are discarded every day.

DOG DIRT BAG DISPENSERS
There are 2,928 dog dirt bag dispensers in Vienna.

HORSE-RIDING AT THE PRATER

Horse-riding at the Prater is only permitted, if the horse carries license plates on both sides of the head harness.

© Wiener Linien / 01.01.1900 Norbert Geiter

THE VIENNA HORSE TRAMWAY

ULTRA LOW FLOOR
From Horse tramways to ULF trams (Ultra Low Floor). The "Wiener Linien" (Vienna Lines) transported over 900 million people in 2012.

Wiener Linien
Erdberg Street 202
1030 Vienna
www.wienerlinien.at

The last horse-tram stopped running on June 26, 1903. The first predecessor of the Vienna tram was the Brigittenauer railway, which was also a horse-tram, operating from July 2, 1840, to June 29, 1842, between Danube channel and the entertainment establishment Kolosseum, which was located at the end of Jäger Street in Brigittenau.

Fishing on the Danube Canal

THE FAUNA OF DANUBE CHANNEL

Danube channel is a retreat for numerous types of fish. There are around 30 different species that are endangered in the Danube river itself.

FISH AT HOME
The farming of fish longer than 3 feet has to be registered with the responsible authority.

VETERINARY MEDICAL UNIVERSITY VIENNA

The "VetMedUni" Vienna was founded in 1765 by Empress Maria Theresa to find cures for cattle diseases. It was the third of its kind in the world, and the first of its kind in the German-speaking region. After 1795, it was called

CAMPUS
There are 47 buildings occupying 15 hectares of land.

"Militair-Thierarzneyschule", which basically means Veterinary School. To this day, the "VetMedUni" remains the only veterinary school in Austria with 2,286 students (as of January 15, 2013).

CLOSED SEASON

While drake mallards, canards and common pochards can neither be traced, captured, or killed from January 16 to August 31, closed season for tufted ducks lasts from February 1 until September 20.

INTIMATE KNOWLEDGE

In Vienna, "Sex, Drugs and Rock'n'Roll" has long been known as "Wine, Women and Song". Vienna has never been a place of abstinence. STADTBEKANNT knows Vienna's most intimate secrets and reveals why you should consider trying the "Vienna Oyster" at home, how dirty classical music can be, and what Bambi's got to do with a prostitute.

Vienna Oyster, Painter Johann Nepomuk Geiger

VIENNA OYSTER

In case you are wondering, the "Vienna Oyster" is a sex position. A watercolor painting of Viennese painter Peter Johann Nepomuk Geiger from 1840 shows two lovers on a sofa. The painting "aroused" the public in many ways – after the exhibition, the "Vienna Oyster" allegedly became one of the most popular sex-positions in Vienna's brothels.

BURGUNDY SNAIL
The Burgundy snail, also known as "Vienna Oyster", was popular because of its aphrodisiac effect.

A NUN FROM VIENNA

On All Saints' Day, in 1753, the famous lover Casanova stole a nun's entire stash of condoms, only to leave behind – being the gentleman that he was – a poem.

VIENNA'S PUNTERS

THE WORLD OF CONDOM
The Condomi Museum explores the history of condoms, ranging from woven bags of cloth to condoms made of sheep intestines and other membranes, to various latex versions.

Every day, 10,000 to 50,000 punters are paying for sex in Vienna. Various estimates suggest that between 5,000 and 10,000 prostitutes, legally or illegally, have around 3 to 5 clients per day.

FELIX SALTEN

OFFSPRING
Both Bambi and Josephine Mutzenbacher had a sequel: "Bambi's Children. A Family in the Woods" and "Peperl Mutzenbacher – The Daughter of Josephine Mutzenbacher".

Felix Salten's children's book "Bambi - A Life in the Woods" made him world famous. He was also the author of the pornographic classic "Josephine Mutzenbacher – The Life Story of a Viennese Whore", written in first-person narrative.

THE NYMPHS OF THE GRABEN

SYNONYMS
Cocotte, Curtisane, Lady of easy virtue, Love servant, Street girl, Pavement princess, Hetaera, Concubine, Mistress, Leg, Broom, Beauty, Belt buckle, Harlot, Easy girl ...

The working zone of the so-called nymphs of the Graben, who offered their services on the Graben in the first district, was marked by chalk lines. That's where the German expression "walk the line" (work the streets) comes from.

PUDERN (TO HAVE SEX)

The word "pudern" comes from "whipping". The technique of whipping cream into butter must have reminded a few people of something.

TSCHURI (SPERM)

"Tschuri" comes from the Romani word "djuuri", which means soup.

VIENNA CLASSIC

"Lick my ass nice and clean" (KV 382d) is a triple canon, not to be confused with "Lick my ass" (KV 382c), which is a different canon for 6 voices by Wolfgang Amadeus Mozart.

GALANT MUSIC AND SENSITIVE STYLE
Wolfgang Amadeus Mozart was a prominent member of the Viennese classicism, which is a style of European art music, combining the so-called Galant music with the so-called Sensitive style.

KOTH (FECAL) STREET – ONCE A POPULAR STREET NAME

Since toilets in mid-evil buildings were often located within projecting alcoves, human excrement was flushed right onto the streets. That's why Blut Street, Pramer Street, as well as Gumpendorfer Street used to be called Koth Street.

FUT (CUNT) ACTUALLY MEANS ASS

The word "Fut" comes from the Middle High German word "vut" and originally stood for butt. It is related to the Alemannic word "füdle", a short version of "fudloch". It was first used for anus and later defined the entire backside.

LINGUISTIC LESSONS

Don't "make a Koarl" of a "Kiebara", otherwise he pulls his "Pretzel" and that's the end of "leiwand". Not even a "Piefke" would understand these words, but we have a solution: "Notify the Ministry of Salt" - or just read this chapter.

WIR HABEN UNS AN KOARL GEMACHT "WE MADE OURSELVES A KOARL"

CARLTHEATER
Carltheater was almost completely destroyed in World War II. Today, the Galaxy Tower stands in its place.

The expression "we made ourselves a Koarl" means to have a great deal of fun and goes all the way back to the Carltheater, which was known for comedies.

A KIEBARA IS KA HABARA "A KIEBARA IS NO HABARA"

This proverb is a reminder that a police officer is not your friend (Habara). A Kiebara (or Kuberer) was a police officer in charge of regulating prostitution. Kuberer comes from the Yiddish word "kübbe", which basically means brothel.

IM LEO SEIN "BEING IN LEO"

PATRON SAINT
St. Leopold is the patron saint of Vienna.

The expression "being in Leo" refers to a safe area. It derives from the Leopold ring on the outside wall of St. Stephan's Cathedral. Whoever made it to the ring was "in Leo" and therefore protected by the church.

VIENNA SHOE

The Vienna shoe is a modification of the Spanish boot. Beware, wearing these shoes wasn't a question of style. The Vienna shoe squashed the foot to the point of bones breaking and/or splinting, while the Spanish

boot squeezed the lower leg until shin- and calve bones were fractured. To increase their potency, both shoes were made out of metal – that way, heating the shoe could provide additional motivation, for the ones wearing it, to speak the truth. This torture instrument was the inspiration for the expression "I werd da de Wadln viererichtn" ("I will set your calves straight").

TORTURE MUSEUM
Situated inside a World War II. bunker, this museum illustrates the history of torture in a bizarre yet humorous way.

Fritz-Grünbaum Square
1060 Vienna

HANDCUFFS

In Vienna, "Eights", "Eight irons" and "Pretzel" are Police jargon for handcuffs.

Jonasreindl

JONASREINDL

JONASGROTTE
JONASWURM
Not just the "Jonasreindl" is named after Franz Jonas. There is also the "Jonasgrotto" (Opera house passage) and the "Jonasworm" (first articulated Vienna tram-way)

The underground tram loop at Schottentor (Schottengate) was built during the term of mayor Franz Jonas. The shape of the loop, along with its ramp leading up to Währinger Street, reminded people of a frying pan, which in Vienna is called a "Reindl". That's how the name "Jonasreindl" came about.

IM SAUWINKEL (PIG'S CORNER)

This street, connecting Post Street and Dominikanerbastei, owes its name to the slaughter house "Im Sauwinkel" originally located there. In 1862, however, it was renamed "Auwinkel" after the natural reserve on the outskirts of Vienna - the Au.

DRINKING MONEY AND GREASE MONEY (TIPS AND BRIBES)

Soon after Mariahilfer Street was renamed Post Street, the first taverns opened. At the same time, tourism started to flourish as traveling by horse-carriage became safer and more comfortable. The German words for "Tip" and "Bribe" originate from those days. Travel books back then listed both these charges as regular fees, along with ticket fees, baggage fees, etc. Drinking money (the tip) was supposed to pay for the driver's drink at a service area. Grease money (the bribe) was collected to grease the wheels of the carriage. If you happened to be in a rush, a larger tip or bribe usually helped "motivate" the driver.

POLICE

The Viennese slang-word "Heh" (Police) derives from Hehmann, a giant spirit of the forest wearing a black coat. He got his name by constantly screaming "Heh". Hehmann punishes thieves stealing wood and is the protector of the forest.

KONRAD POPPENBERGER
In 1425, the City of Vienna purchased the "Rear Women's House" from Konrad Poppenberger. It was a business enterprise, a brothel to be exact, which paid for relatives of poorly regarded members of society like police officers or executioners.

KRIEAU

The name "Krieau" derives from "Kriegsau" (War Au), because of a territorial dispute between the Diocese Klosterneuburg and the City of Vienna, which lasted for decades.

LETTER SOUP
Krieau – 4 different vowels in a row!

Lobau

LOBAU

The name "Lobau" comes from the Old High German word "lo", which means dense forest.

BESERLPARK (BROOM PARK)

GREEN VIENNA
There are about 250 parks in Vienna.

A park was once built at the Franz-Josefs-Kai. Since the trees there weren't properly taken care of, they started to look like brooms. That's why the park is called "Beserlpark".

Friedhof

ROLAND NEUWIRTH / „EIN ECHTES WIENERLIED“ (A TRADITIONAL VIENNESE SONG)“

This song by Austrian composer and musician Robert Neuwirth is famous for exclusively using Viennese slang words for dying. The combination of humor and morbidity makes it a truly, traditional Viennese song.

He made an exit,
He stretched his feet,
He tore down a bench,
He laid down,

VIENNA AND DEATH
One of the reasons for Vienna's obsession with death, could be the fact that the number of dead people in Vienna is far greater than the number of people alive. Three million people alone are buried at Vienna's Zentralfriedhof (Central cemetery).

SCHRAMMEL MUSIC (VIENNESE FOLK MUSIC)
Schrammel music is named after the brothers Johann and Josef Schrammel. Both brothers died at the age of 43.

He looked at potatoes from below,
He slipped into the wooden pyjama,
He set up a stand,
He notched the hoofs,
He gave himself the noose,
He took the step,
He stood around,
He bent it,
The poor pig ended up at St. Peter's.

He descended, as they say,
He went to see if the lid fits,
They carried him out feet first,
Now, he's laughing at worms instead of girls.

Inside Ruprechts Church, the Ministry of Salt sold salt to retailers.

LANGUAGES

100 different languages are spoken in Vienna.

LEIWAND (GREAT/COOL/FANTASTIC)

In the 15th century, the Bürgerspital (citizen's hospital) became an international hub for the textile trade. The beer, served to the bargaining merchants, was soon called "Leinwandbier", referring to the "Leinenhandel" (linen trade) going on there. The beer was tasty and quickly established a good reputation. That's how the word "leiwand" (great/cool/fantastic) was born.

BEER - WINE
In 1732, the people of Vienna drank three times as much wine as they drank beer. In 2012, beer was consumed four times as much as wine.

PIEFKE (DEROGATORY WORD FOR GERMAN PEOPLE)

PIEFKE-MEMORIAL
To commemorate Johann Gottfried Piefke, the Piefke-Memorial was built in Gänserndorf in September 2009.

In 1866, a parade in Gänserndorf celebrated the Prussian victory over Austria. Among the conductors back then was Johann Gottfried Piefke, a name that would become proverbial.

SALZAMT (MINISTRY OF SALT)

Until 1824, Vienna's Ministry of Salt was located at the Prague House, next to Ruprechts Church. After the ministry was closed, the building stood vacant until 1832 and was considered a "ministry without function". That's how the Viennese expression "Notify the Ministry of Salt" came about. (It basically means "to stop complaining, because nobody will listen")

TRÖPFERLBAD (DRIPPING BATHHOUSES)

FLORABAD
The Wieden District Museum is located inside a former "Tröpferlbad", the Florabad on Klagbaum Street 4.

The first public bathhouse in Europe opened its gates in Vienna in 1887. There was such a rush that the water supply system collapsed. Showers were merely dripping. Since then, public swimming pools are commonly known as "Tröpferlbäder".

facebook.com/Raum66

K·K·HO
Buchhandlung
Leporello

JUST NONSENSE

True greatness has no limits, which is why there is no end to useless information about Vienna. Anything not worth knowing about Vienna, is gathered in this last chapter. As an added bonus, STADTBEKANNT has thrown in a few useful facts here and there. For example: What the light signals on top of the Ring Tower mean, why a Viennese box might come in handy, or where to really find the Sigmund Freud Museum.

The Au Garden

THE AU GARDEN: THE GEOGRAPHICAL CENTER OF VIENNA

The STADTBEKANNT task force has located and marked the geographical center of Vienna. The coordinates are 48.220282, 16.3800575. It is located on the southern edge of the Au Garden.

FLAK TOWERS
The two flak towers at the Au Garden are codenamed Peter.

BARON KARL

Baron-Karl Street in Favoriten wasn't named after an aristocrat, but a popular homeless man by the name of Karl Baron. Baron was simply his last name. It is said that over 10,000 people attended his funeral.

DISTRICT GRAMMAR

Districts 1 to 4, 8, 20 and 22 are female and have an article. Districts 7 and 9 are male and also have an article. Districts 5, 6, 10 to 19, 21 and 23 are neuter and do not have an article.

SUICIDE

WOMEN ARE DIFFERENT – MEN TOO!
Men and women apparently do have things in common. For both sexes, death by hanging is by far the most popular way to commit suicide.

December and January are the months with the fewest suicides – especially during Christmas holidays, people rarely take their own lives. Vienna has one of the lowest suicide rates in Austria.

ST. STEPHAN'S CATHEDRAL

There is a numeric symbolism behind the measurements of St. Stephan's Cathedral. It consists of the numbers Three and Four. Three symbolizes the Holy Trinity, while Four stands for the four cardinal directions. Together, they add up to Seven, which correlates with the Seven sacraments, the Seven virtues, the Seven sins, the Seven days of Creation, etc. These three numbers are repeatedly found in the metrics of the Cathedral.

IMPERIAL HOTEL

SCULLION
The Sacher-Torte and the Imperial-Torte were both invented by a scullions.

If you stay at the Vienna Imperial Hotel, you may list 4 different addresses: Kärntnerring 16, Bösendorfer Street 15, Dumba Street 1, and Canova Street 2.

BERG STREET 19, NOT BURG STREET 19!

SIGMUND FREUD
Museums, monuments, paper bills, and stamps commemorate Sigmund Freud. Not only schools, universities, institutes and professorships are named after him, an asteroid and a crater on the moon also carry his name.

Numerous tourists end up on Burg Street 19, expecting to find the Sigmund Freud Museum, actually located on Berg Street 19. For a while now, a Freud caricature inside a window apologizes to the lost tourists. "Sorry! This is not my former home! Your guide is wrong! You have to go to Berggasse 19!" P.S: "Maybe some patients live here . . ."

Prater

THE SIZE OF THE PRATER

The Prater is about twice as large as Central Park in New York.

STREET OF WINNERS

164 athletes received a sidewalk plaque on the street of winners on Mariahilfer Street. Among them, Hansi Hinterseer, who is the only one also immortalized on the "Walk of Stars" at the Gasometer.

CONSERVATION

Around 30 percent of Vienna is protected land.

GREEN AREA
Green areas occupy one half of Vienna.

THE OLDEST BRIDGE IN VIENNA

VIENNA BRIDGES
The length of all the bridges in Vienna combined is 33 miles.

The oldest bridge is the Konstantinsteg built in 1873. The bridge is still in use at the Vienna Prater.

VIENNA'S REVERSED STREET

Fred-Liewehr Street in Speising is the only street in Vienna with reverse street numbers. Here, the odd numbers are on the right side.

NATURAL LANDMARK

The "one-thousand-year-old" yew tree at the European Patent Office on Rennweg, is the oldest, botanical natural landmark in Vienna.

The public restroom on the Graben

PUBLIC RESTROOM ON THE GRABEN

The public restroom on the Graben is Vienna's oldest toilet facility. It once offered first and second class "seating".

COMFORT STATION
There are 302 public restrooms in Vienna. The most frequented public restroom is the one at the Rathaus Park with around 400,000 visitors per year.

LONGEST AND SHORTEST STREETS IN VIENNA

With 8.7 miles, Höhen Street is the longest street in Vienna. The shortest street is Iris Street at only 55 feet in length.

THE "WIENER LINIEN" CIRCLE THE PLANET

TRAMWAY MUSEUM
The Vienna Tramway Museum, which explores the advancement of public transport, hosts a comprehensive collection of historical tramways and buses. For more information, please visit: www.wienerlinien.at

Last year, the "Wiener Linien" circled the earth 1,650 times. Subway, trams, and buses cover about 111,000 miles each day. That's 41 million miles per year, equaling 1,650 circumnavigations.

GENERAL HOSPITAL

Slight miscalculation: The construction of the AKH (General hospital) was projected to cost 1 billion ATS and ended up swallowing 45 billion ATS.

VIENNA GÜRTEL (BELT)

STADTBAHNBÖGEN (VIADUCT ARCHES ALONG THE GÜRTEL)
There are 365 "Stadtbahnbögen" in Vienna.

In 2006, over 40 % of all apartments around the Gürtel didn't have a toilet.

DONAUTURM (DANUBE TOWER)

The two elevators inside the Danube Tower covered a distance of around 466,000 miles between 1964 and 2010 – that equals a trip to the moon and back.

FOOD SAFETY COMMISSION

Every year, the food safety commission pays 13,000 unannounced visits to businesses across Vienna.

Flak Tower

VIENNA FLAK TOWERS

The Vienna Flak towers vary in height. The platforms on top, however, are all on the exact same sea-level.

AKH VIENNA GENERAL HOSPITAL

There are 6,500 intercoms, 7,500 telephones for employees, and 1,000 phones for patients at the AKH.

TRANSPLANTATION
Doctors at the AKH were the first in the world to successfully perform a tongue transplant.

PATHOLOGY

The Vienna Pathology is located on Sensen Street 2 in the 9th district.

VIENNA FIRE DEPARTMENT

The response time of the Vienna Fire Department is 30 seconds during the day and 60 seconds at night time.

HOCHSTRAHL FOUNTAIN SYMBOLISM

VIENNA FOUNTAINS
In Vienna, more than 700 drinking fountains offer refreshment. The Vienna drinking fountain, invented by Hans Muhr, can also be found in Berlin, Budapest, Chicago, Geneva, Hongkong, Leipzig and Stockholm.

The beautiful "Hochstrahlbrunnen" on Schwarzenberg Square knows all types of calenders. 365 small fountains on the edge of the basin symbolize the days of the year. The six fountains in between the edge of the basin and the inner island, including the one on the inner island, correlate with the 7 days of the week. The 12 high jets symbolize the 12 months, the 24 lower jets the hours of the day. The 30 jets on the central island stand for the days in a month.

VIENNA MUNICIPALITY BUILDINGS

LIVING IN VIENNA
Around 855,000 apartments in Vienna are rented out. 80,000 flats are vacant. Each year, around 50,000 leases are signed.

The massive Karl-Marx-Hof is almost 4,000 feet, or 4 tram stops, long. It contains 1,325 apartments with 98 stairs covering an area of 1.7 million square feet. However, in terms of units it is only ranked third. Number 2 is Residential Estate Friedrich-Engels Square with 1,467 apartments,

The High Bridge

47 stairs and 737,000 square feet. Residential Estate Sandleiten is number 1 with 1,534 apartments, 105 stairs and 817,000 square feet.

VIENNA RING STREET

Ring Street is numbered clock-wise. Only the Kärnterring is numbered counter clock-wise.

RING STREET
Ring Street is almost 200 feet wide and 2.5 miles long.

VIENNA WOODS STREAMS

27 streams from the Vienna Woods run through Vienna. Some of them are invisible. The Ottakringer Stream for example, the second longest stream, runs entirely underground.

VIENNA WOODS STREAMS
Long ago, around 70 streams were running through the City of Vienna.

HOTEL STEFANIE

Hotel Stefanie located on Tabor Street is the oldest hotel in Vienna.

THE HIGH BRIDGE

LOTTERY
"Cross the High Bridge and get lucky" was the advertising slogan of a lottery branch on the High Bridge

The high bridge in the first district crosses "Tiefen Graben". The buildings on "Tiefen Graben" are basically the basements of the buildings on Wipplinger Street, which crosses "Tiefen Graben".

VIENNA INTERNATIONAL CENTER

VIC
The Vienna International Center's postal code is 1400.

The Vienna International Center has 24,000

windows.

ARGENTINIER STREET

Before Argentinier Street received its South American name, it had many others: The area was previously called "Haferpoint", after 1700 it was called Allee Street, and in 1862 it was renamed Sophien Street. Today's name commemorates the 5-million-Peso donation, Argentine made to Austria after World War I.

ART HISTORY MUSEUM

On the roof of the Art History Museum, there is a statue of Pallas Athene, goddess of wisdom and the arts.

ART HISTORY MUSEUM
Burgring 5, 1010 Vienna
www.khm.at

THE "VIENNA" SCHWECHAT

During the construction of the airport expressway, the river Schwechat had to be re-regulated. Since then, the river runs exclusively through the State of Lower Austria.

VIENNA GARBAGE

12 % of Vienna's garbage consists of unopened or partially opened foods – that's 70,000 tons per year. To transport this amount of "garbage", 11,500 garbage trucks are needed.

The Man of City Hall

VIENNA BOXES

A Vienna box is a wallet that opens like a collapsible box.

THE MAN OF CITY HALL

The "Iron Man of City Hall" is made of copper.

Saint

VIENNA AND ITS SAINTS

Vienna is under double protection. St. Leopold is the patron saint of the State of Vienna. St. Clemens Maria Hofbauer is the patron saint of the City of Vienna.

WORLD MEN'S DAY

VIENNA POPULATION
In 2013, there were 1,731,236 people living in Vienna. 900,299 women vs. 830,937 men.

The 3rd of November is World Men's Day. The idea came from andrologists at the University of Vienna in 2000. Andrology is the medical specialty that deals with male health, particularly relating to problems that are unique to men.

EICHKOGEL

The "Eichkogel" is the highest mountain of the 23rd district at 1,400 feet.

HABE-DIE-EHRE STREET (GOOD DAY STREET)

The most polite street in Vienna has to be Habe-die-Ehre Street in the 22nd district. The phrase literally translates to "Having the Honor" and is still used as a form of greeting.

RING TOWER

VIENNA WEATHER
The average air temperature in Vienna is 11 degrees Celsius (52 degrees Fahrenheit).

There is a 60-foot weather-station on top of the Ring Tower. Lights of different colors announce the weather for the coming days. The light pillar is connected to ZAMG (Central Institution for Meteorology and Geodynamics) and the weather station at the Hohe Warte.
Meaning of light signals:
red ascending = temperature rising
red descending = temperature falling
green ascending = weather condition improving

Wien River

green descending = weather condition worsening
red flashing = Thunderstorm or storm warning
white flashing = snow and/or icy roads

WIEN RIVER

The Wien river runs along 9 districts: Innere Stadt, Landstraße, Wieden, Margareten, Mariahilf, Meidling, Hietzing, Penzing, Rudolfsheim-Fünfhaus. It separates the four districts on the left side of the river, from the five districts on the right side.

VIENNA WOODS STREAMS
The Wien river is one of 27 Vienna Woods streams that runs through Vienna.

TOM TURBO'S HEADQUARTERS

Tom Turbo's headquarters are located at the

THOMAS BREZINA
Thomas Brezina wrote around 480 books in the last twenty years. That's two books per month! Some of his books were translated into 35 languages.

Vienna Zoo, right next to the tortoises.

LUDWIG VON DRAKE

Ludwig von Drake, one of Walt Disney's characters, was originally from Vienna.

WALULISO

This Viennese original's message was peace. WALULISO stands for WAsser. LUft, LIcht und SOnne. (water, air, light and sun). The Waluliso Bridge connects the "Donauinsel" with the Hubertus dam.